GEISINGER

Geisinger Clinic is a multispecialty physician group practice with nearly 650 physicians located in central and northeastern Pennsylvania. The clinic's mission is "to enhance the quality of life through an integrated health service organization based on a balanced program of patient care, education, research, and community service." This mission is summarized: **"Heal. Teach. Discover. Serve."**

To learn more about the Geisinger Healthcare System visit www.geisinger.org

FAQs * SERIES

Also in this series

---

*Frequently Asked Questions

RHEUMATOID ARTHRITIS

GEISINGER

FAQs

Author

Eric D. Newman, MD

Cynthia K. Matzko, RN, MSN

Series Editor

Sandra A. Buckley

2007

BC Decker Inc

Hamilton

BC Decker Inc
P.O. Box 620, L.C.D. 1
Hamilton, Ontario L8N 3K7
Tel: 905-522-7017; 800-568-7281
Fax: 905-522-7839; 888-311-4987
E-mail: info@bcdecker.com
www.bcdecker.com

07 08 09/PI/9 8 7 6 5 4 3 2 1

ISBN 1-55009-341-X
Printed in Canada

Sales and Distribution

United States
BC Decker Inc
P.O. Box 785
Lewiston, NY 14092-0785
Tel: 905-522-7017; 800-568-7281
Fax: 905-522-7839; 888-311-4987
E-mail: info@bcdecker.com
www.bcdecker.com

Canada
BC Decker Inc
50 King St. E.
P.O. Box 620, LCD 1
Hamilton, Ontario L8N 3K7
Tel: 905-522-7017; 800-568-7281
Fax: 905-522-7839; 888-311-4987
E-mail: info@bcdecker.com
www.bcdecker.com

Foreign Rights
John Scott & Company
International Publishers' Agency
P.O. Box 878
Kimberton, PA 19442
Tel: 610-827-1640
Fax: 610-827-1671
E-mail: jsco@voicenet.com

Japan
Igaku-Shoin Ltd.
Foreign Publications Department
3-24-17 Hongo
Bunkyo-ku, Tokyo, Japan 113-8719
Tel: 3 3817 5680
Fax: 3 3815 6776
E-mail: fd@igaku-shoin.co.jp

UK, Europe, Scandinavia,
Middle East
Elsevier Science
UK, Europe, Scandinavia, Middle
East, Africa
Elsevier Ltd.
Books Customer Services
Linacre House
Jordan Hill
Oxford
OX2 8DP, UK
Tel: 44 (0) 1865 474 010
Fax: 44 (0) 1865 474 011
E-mail: eurobkinfo@elsevier.com

Singapore, Malaysia,Thailand,
Philippines, Indonesia, Vietnam,
Pacific Rim, Korea
Elsevier Science Asia
583 Orchard Road
#09/01, Forum
Singapore 238884
Tel: 65-737-3593
Fax: 65-753-2145

Australia, New Zealand
Elsevier Science Australia
Customer Service Department
Locked Bag 16
St. Peters, New South Wales 2044
Australia
Tel: 61 02-9517-8999
Fax: 61 02-9517-2249
E-mail:
customerserviceau@elsevier.com
www.elsevier.com.au

Mexico and Central America
ETM SA de CV
Calle de Tula 59
Colonia Condesa
06140 Mexico DF, Mexico
Tel: 52-5-5553-6657
Fax: 52-5-5211-8468
E-mail:
editoresdetextosmex@prodigy.net.mx

Brazil
Tecmedd Importadora E Distribuidora
De Livros Ltda.
Avenida Maurílio Biagi, 2850
City Ribeirão, Ribeirão Preto – SP –
Brasil
CEP: 14021-000
Tel: 0800 992236
Fax: (16) 3993-9000
E-mail: tecmedd@tecmedd.com.br

India, Bangladesh, Pakistan,
Sri Lanka
Elsevier Health Sciences Division
Customer Service Department
17A/1, Main Ring Road
Lajpat Nagar IV
New Delhi – 110024, India
Tel: 91 11 2644 7160-64
Fax: 91 11 2644 7156
E-mail: esindia@vsnl.net

Acknowledgments

The authors would like to thank John Foster LPT, Susan Pannebaker MSW, and Kathy Boudeman RD CDE LDN for their contributions.

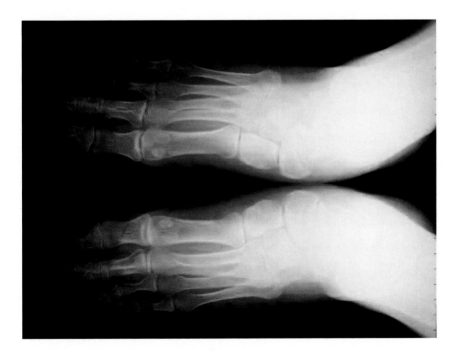

Dedication

To Laurie, Nathaniel, and Alyssa—for your inspiration, love, and support

and

To Michael, Michelle, and Michael—for your love and encouragement.

About this Book

This book was developed to address frequently asked questions (FAQs) about rheumatoid arthritis. We hope this book will help people with rheumatoid arthritis (and their families) understand the disease and its treatment.

Contents

CHAPTER ONE

What is Arthritis?
What is Rheumatoid Arthritis?

Arthritis is any condition that changes the joint or interferes with joint motion. More than 100 types of arthritis exist and inflammation is sometimes involved. It's important for you to know what type of arthritis you have. Once you understand your arthritis, you'll better understand how it will be treated.

What does inflammation have to do with arthritis?

Inflammation is your body's way of protecting itself and helping heal an injured area. For example, if you were hit on the arm with a baseball, your arm would become red, hot, swollen, painful, and uncomfortable to move. This is a normal inflammatory response. It happens quickly and goes away after a short period of time. But if the inflammation doesn't come as a result of an injury or other outside trauma and if its symptoms last too long, it will damage that part.

Some types of arthritis are caused by inflammation. How much inflammation and where it is depends on the type of arthritis. Symptoms of inflammation are redness, heat, swelling, pain, stiffness, and difficulty moving the inflamed area.

So inflammation isn't present with all types of arthritis?

No. Most forms of arthritis fall into two basic categories:

- Inflammatory and
- Noninflammatory

The most common *noninflammatory arthritis* is *osteoarthritis* (degenerative joint disease) a condition caused from cartilage becoming worn down (Figure 1-1). When cartilage wears down, its surface changes from smooth to irregular. Damaged cartilage isn't a good shock absorber and causes discomfort with movement. Bone spurs (bony projections that form along joints) may develop and fluid may accumulate in the joint. Osteoarthritis tends to occur the older we become but can occur because of a previous injury to the joint or obesity (both factors increase the stress on a joint). The major joint problems due to osteoarthritis are pain and decreased motion. Osteoarthritis can affect any joint but the most common are the knees, hips, spine, and hands.

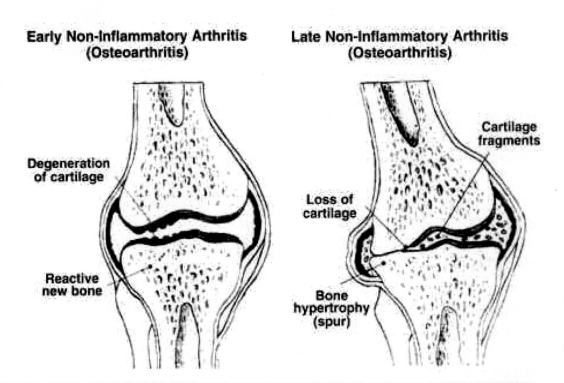

Figure 1-1. *A,* Early noninflammatory arthritis (osteoarthritis). *B,* Late noninflammatory arthritis (osteoarthritis).

Inflammatory arthritis (Figure 1-2) means the joints, the lining of the joint, and surrounding tissues are inflamed. This inflammation usually doesn't go away if it isn't treated or isn't treated properly. Over time, the inflamed lining can cause significant joint damage.

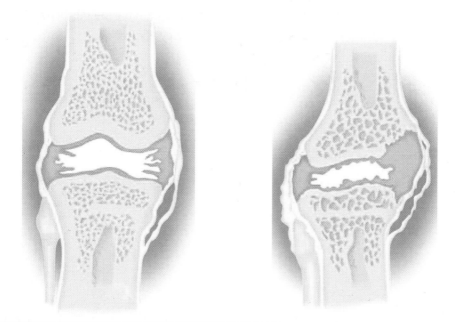

Figure 1-2. *A*, Early inflammatory arthritis (rheumatoid arthritis). *B*, Late inflammatory arthritis (rheumatoid arthritis).

Is rheumatoid arthritis inflammatory or noninflammatory?

Rheumatoid arthritis is the most common form of inflammatory arthritis. It is a *chronic* disease—one that lasts for a long time. If you have rheumatoid arthritis, it usually "flares up" and your pain increases during these flare-ups. Pain decreases when inflammation is controlled. The better the disease is controlled, the less pain you will have. You'll see later in this book how you and your doctor can establish the correct diet, exercise, and medications to ease inflammation and control your pain.

Q

A

What are the signs and symptoms of rheumatoid arthritis?

Signs and symptoms of rheumatoid arthritis include stiffness, fatigue, pain, limited joint motion, joint swelling, and warm and red joints. People with rheumatoid arthritis experience a great deal of stiffness and difficulty moving, especially in the morning and after sitting for a long time. Joints may ache with nagging pain causing you to be uncomfortable. Enough joint pain and damage can make you unable to perform routine daily activities. A feeling of tiredness can sometimes be overpowering.

CHAPTER TWO

Which Parts of the Body Are Affected by Rheumatoid Arthritis?

Generally, the joints most frequently involved in rheumatoid arthritis are the hands, wrists, knees, and feet, but any joint could be affected.

How do joints work?

Joints connect your *bones* (the major support structure for the body) and let your body move. Normal body motion—walking, buttoning a blouse, swinging a baseball bat, or threading a needle—requires joints that work normally (Figure 2-1). Cartilage, a sponge-like material, covers the ends of bones and acts as a shock absorber when joints move. *Synovial membrane* lines the joint. It makes fluid for the cartilage and lubricates the joint (like oil does for machinery), protecting the joint and permitting smooth movement. *Tendons* connect muscle to joints, providing power for joints to move. *Ligaments* connect bone to bone, providing stability to the joint and preventing too much joint movement. The *joint capsule* surrounds the joint and adds to joint stability.

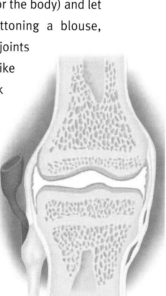

Figure 2-1. Normal joint.

What happens to the joints when you have rheumatoid arthritis?

Basically, the synovial membrane (described in the previous answer) thickens, secretes more fluid, and the joint swells. This is known as synovitis. If the synovitis is not controlled, the joints can begin to deteriorate.

Does rheumatoid arthritis only affect the joints?

No, rheumatoid arthritis can affect other body parts too. You might have nodules (lumps) that form around the joint areas. You might have dry eyes and a dry mouth from certain inflammatory "fighting" cells that clog the saliva and tear ducts. You might have inflammation of the lung tissues (called *pulmonary fibrosis*), lumps in the lungs (pulmonary nodules), and fluid around the lungs (pleural effusion). Inflammation of the sac that surrounds the heart (*pericarditis*) may occur. Sometimes swelling at the wrist or ankle may pinch the nerves and cause numbness of the fingers or toes.

Are these complications common?

It's not that these complications are very uncommon, it's just that everyone's body reacts differently with rheumatoid arthritis. Some complications, however, are very rare. These include inflammation of the heart and nodules on the heart valves, damage to the spinal cord at the level of the neck, or inflammation of blood vessels that can damage the organ or body part that receives blood from those vessels. A very rare condition, called Felty's syndrome, occurs in about 1–2% of all patients. This condition consists of a combination of rheumatoid arthritis, an enlarged spleen, and a very low white blood count. Some people with Felty's syndrome will have recurring infections that can be life threatening.

Can rheumatoid arthritis affect the rest of my overall health?

Yes. Because rheumatoid arthritis affects multiple body parts, it can lead to the complications we just described. Early diagnosis and appropriate treatment are very important. You might need only minimal therapy or you might have to see experts in several different fields if your rheumatoid arthritis requires more aggressive treatment to decrease joint pain, joint damage, and disability.

CHAPTER THREE

What Causes Rheumatoid Arthritis?

More than two million people in the United States suffer from rheumatoid arthritis—that's about 2 out of every 100 adults.

Do we know what causes rheumatoid arthritis?

Not exactly. In fact, there probably isn't one specific cause of rheumatoid arthritis. What we do know is that the body's immune system plays an important role in rheumatoid arthritis. Rheumatoid arthritis is known as an *autoimmune disease* because if you have rheumatoid arthritis, it means you have an abnormal immune system response.

What does rheumatoid arthritis have to do with the immune system?

The immune system usually works this way: immune cells in your body help to protect you from outside foreign substances. If you have rheumatoid arthritis, your immune system "revs up" without having a foreign substance to defend against.

Does gender influence getting rheumatoid arthritis?

Researchers do believe that gender might play some role in how rheumatoid arthritis develops and progresses. Rheumatoid arthritis affects nearly twice as many women than men, usually between the ages of 25 and 50, although any age (including children) can be affected. Researchers are trying to understand what role female hormones might play. Interestingly, women with rheumatoid arthritis usually go into *remission* (a period of time where symptoms of a disease are not present) when they are pregnant. Also, women tend to develop rheumatoid arthritis in the year after pregnancy and symptoms of rheumatoid arthritis can increase the year after giving birth.

Does rheumatoid arthritis run in families?

It might. Rheumatoid arthritis is not an inherited disease, although you can inherit the genes that make you more likely to develop it.

Rheumatoid Arthritis: Where Does It Come From?
- The body's immune system plays an important role
- More women than men get it
- You might inherit genes that make you more likely to develop it

CHAPTER FOUR

How is Rheumatoid Arthritis Diagnosed?

We described the signs and symptoms of rheumatoid arthritis in Chapter 1, but merely having these signs and symptoms doesn't mean you have rheumatoid arthritis. You'll need to see a doctor for a true diagnosis of rheumatoid arthritis.

How can I be tested for rheumatoid arthritis?

Blood tests can be used to help diagnose rheumatoid arthritis. Blood often shows mild *anemia* (low red blood count) and increased *platelet* count (platelets are necessary to help the blood clot). These symptoms are a result of the body's reaction to inflammation. The *blood rheumatoid factor* (an antibody that is not usually present in a normal individual) is often elevated. About half of patients with early rheumatoid arthritis show a positive rheumatoid factor. About 80% of patients who have had rheumatoid arthritis for a number of years will have a positive rheumatoid factor. The rheumatoid factor can be a bit misleading, though. Some patients who *do* have rheumatoid arthritis *do not* have a positive rheumatoid factor. However, many other conditions can cause an elevated rheumatoid factor, so having or not having rheumatoid factor does *not* confirm the diagnosis of rheumatoid arthritis.

A relatively new test (*anti-cyclic citrullinated peptide*) may indicate rheumatoid arthritis. It can be detected in patients even before the rheumatoid factor becomes positive.

Ultimately, the diagnosis of rheumatoid arthritis is made based on a combination of clinical signs and symptoms, laboratory studies, and x-rays. Because of the importance of properly diagnosing and treating rheumatoid arthritis, as well as the fact that there are many other types of inflammating arthritis that can look like rheumatoid arthritis, evaluation by a specially trained physician is important.

Diagnosis: Rheumatoid Arthritis
- Blood tests often show mild anemia and increased platelet count
- Blood rheumatoid factor is usually (but not always) elevated
- Anti-cyclic citrullinated peptide test can detect rheumatoid arthritis even before the blood rheumatoid factor becomes positive

---

When should I see a doctor?

You should see your doctor as soon as you have joint pain that seems out of the ordinary. With rheumatoid arthritis, it is important to make a correct diagnosis and begin treatment. Getting treatment early can help prevent joint damage.

What kinds of doctors treat rheumatoid arthritis?

The doctor best trained to diagnose and treat rheumatoid arthritis is a *rheumatologist*—a specialist in *rheumatology*. Rheumatology is the study of conditions with pain and other symptoms related to the musculoskeletal (bone and muscle) system. The rheumatologist and possibly a rheumatology nurse will work with your primary care doctor to diagnose and manage the disease.

Will I have to see other kinds of health care providers?

Maybe. You might need the care and services of other health care specialists such as physical therapists, occupational therapists, social workers, nutritional experts and orthopedists (bone surgeons).

CHAPTER FIVE

How is Rheumatoid Arthritis Treated?

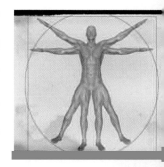

Medical science has made tremendous advances in our ability to care for patients. Many of the newer treatments are targeted—they fix only what needs to be fixed—and are more effective. Expanded choices are now available that can significantly improve the outcome of patients with rheumatoid arthritis—less pain, stiffness, and swelling; more energy; increased joint function; and a better ability to work and enjoy life.

I don't have pain all the time. Is this normal in rheumatoid arthritis?

Yes. When you have arthritis, you have a certain amount of discomfort or pain. Sometimes you feel better than other times. When the arthritis flares up, you feel worse. When it is controlled, you feel better. Your doctor will help you decrease pain by controlling your arthritis.

But before we talk about how your doctor can help, let's discuss how you can help decrease your own pain! Here's what you should know about your pain:

- **The amount or type of pain you have depends on your disease or physical problem.** The pain of rheumatoid arthritis is mostly due to the amount of inflammation located in and around the joints. This causes the joints to be "achy," "stiff and sore," "worse in the morning," and the pain differs from day to day depending on the amount of inflammation present. The less inflammation, the less pain you will have.

- **Your emotional state when you are having pain affects your pain level.** Different emotions lead to different descriptions of pain. For example, if you were having pain on a day you were otherwise happy, you might describe the pain as less severe than on a day you were feeling down or sad. Depression tends to make pain feel worse. Sadness makes you think more about how awful you feel rather than focusing on things happening around you. If you focus your attention on how much it hurts, you will feel the hurt more. If you focus your attention on other people or happenings around you, your mind can be distracted from the pain.

- **Stress is your body's way of defending itself.** When you're stressed, your muscles tighten, your heart rate increases, you breathe more rapidly, and you're mentally alarmed. Some stress is healthy, but too much stress over a prolonged time is unhealthy and may actually cause you to feel more pain. Learning how to cope with things that trigger stress will help you control the amount of pain you experience. You'll read about this more in Chapter 6.

- **Your social and cultural background may affect your pain.** Why? You were brought up learning what was supposed to hurt and how you should respond. For example, in some cultures, pain is felt but not expressed. In other cultures, pain is expressed with shouting and crying. Some people are socialized not to feel pain (such as fire walkers). Have you ever met people who could take a lot of pain? Have you also known people who complained of pain a great deal? What is painful to one may not be painful to another, and because we're all individuals, we must respect and acknowledge this variation in pain.

- **Environmental conditions can affect pain.** People with arthritis often say their pain varies according to the weather. A change in the barometric pressure may be the reason. Ongoing research may one day provide us with additional insight regarding the relationship between arthritis pain and the environment.

What can I take to control the pain I have?

As we just said, people experience different types and amounts of pain. You might find one (or more) of the following methods helpful in decreasing pain:

- Apply heat to the affected area
- Apply cold to the affected area
- Apply a combination of heat and cold
- Take medication

When should I apply heat? How should I do it?

Use heat if your joints are stiff and sore. Heat decreases stiffness because it increases circulation to the area and relaxes muscles around the joint. You can take a warm bath or shower, use a heating pad, or use heat-producing skin lotions. Use heat with caution though. Keep the temperature warm but not so hot that it will burn you. Use heat for 5 to 10 minutes at a time. Never lay directly on top of a heating pad. Always place a cloth between your skin and the heat source. Use the chemical source of heat found in some arthritis lotions only with your doctor's advice and never use these when you are using the heating pad.

When should I apply cold? How should I do it?

Use cold if joints are swollen or have a great deal of pain. The cold reduces swelling and provides a numbing effect that reduces pain. Use cold packs 5 to 10 minutes at a time but as often as you like. You can buy cold packs or make your own. To make a cold pack, place ice in a plastic bag. Then place the ice pack in a cloth and place it on your painful joint. The Arthritis Foundation has also suggested using frozen bags of peas or corn instead of ice because it conforms to the joint.

How do I alternate heat and cold?

Some people with arthritis use 10 minutes of cold, followed by 10 minutes of heat. This technique is called a *contrast bath* and may be helpful if you have severe arthritis flare-up in a joint.

What types of pain medication can I take?

Rheumatoid arthritis can be effectively controlled with medications and is usually treated with a combination of medicines. You may need to take two or three different arthritis medicines to give you the most benefit. These medications fall into four categories:

- Analgesics (pain relief medications)
- Nonsteroidal anti-inflammatory drugs (NSAIDs)
- Steroids (corticosteroids) and
- Slow-acting anti-rheumatic drugs (SAARDs)

A variety of medicines are available within each category. Your doctor will prescribe the arthritis medicine (or medicines) you should take and can change your arthritis medicines if he or she thinks another medicine combination might work better.

What are analgesics?

Analgesics are medicines that relieve pain. They work by blocking the pain message from being interpreted by your brain. Acetaminophen (Tylenol®) is the most commonly used medicine to control the pain of osteoarthritis (degenerative arthritis). However, it is not the primary treatment for active rheumatoid arthritis because it does not control inflammation and is, at best, a helpful *additional* medicine.

If you do take acetaminophen, though, learn the instructions for taking it properly and always take only the recommended dose. If you have pain that Tylenol® does not help, ask your doctor what other options you have. Other analgesic medicines (such as Wygesic® or Darvocet®) are sometimes prescribed. If you have longstanding rheumatoid arthritis that is no longer very inflammatory, but have significant joint damage causing pain, your doctor might prescribe a narcotic.

Do analgesics have side effects?

Side effects from Tylenol® are not common. Low dose Tylenol® seems to be tolerated by most people, however, please follow the directions on the box and your doctor's recommendation.

What are nonsteroidal, anti-inflammatory drugs (NSAIDs)?

NSAIDs decrease arthritis symptoms—pain and inflammation. But some work better in one person than another. It usually takes 2 to 4 weeks of taking an NSAID daily to know how well it will help you. As you might imagine, skipping doses will decrease effectiveness. Your doctor will help you find the NSAID that works best for you (Table 5-1).

Do NSAIDS have side effects?

Major side effects of NSAIDs include an upset stomach, ulcer disease, reduction in kidney function, and rash. You may be able to decrease stomach symptoms by taking your NSAID medication with meals. If you have a history of ulcer disease you may not be able to take NSAIDs; discuss this with your doctor. Other risks that may increase the chance of an ulcer and/or stomach bleed include your age, history of a previous bleeding disorder, use of blood thinning medications (such as Coumadin), and use of steroids (such as Prednisone). Warning signs include heartburn, indigestion, stomach burning, bowel movements that are dark or black, and tiredness. You may not be able to take NSAIDs. Discuss this with your doctor.

You should know, however, ulcers and bleeding can occur without any warning signs whatsoever.

Although NSAIDs rarely cause kidney problems, your doctor may recommend blood and urine tests. NSAIDs may also cause high blood pressure and fluid retention.

Table 5-1: Some Common NSAIDs?

Generic Name	Trade Name
Aspirin	Anacin®, Ascriptin®, Bayer®, Bufferin®, Ecotrin®, Zorprin®
Choline Magnesium Trisalicylate	Trilisate®
Diclofenac sodium	Voltaren®
Diflusinal	Dolobid®
Etodolac	Lodine®
Fenoprofen calcium	Nalfon®
Flurbiprofen	Ansaid®
Ibuprofen	Advil®, Motrin®, Nuprin®
Indomethacin	Indocin®
Ketoprofen	Orudis®
Meclofenamate sodium	Meclomen®
Meloxicam	Mobic®
Nabumetone	Relafen®
Naproxen	Naprosyn®
Naproxen Sodium	Anaprox®
Oxaprozin	DayPro®
Piroxicam	Feldene®
Salsalate	Disalcid®
Sulindac	Clinoril®
Tolmetin sodium	Tolectin®

NSAIDs=nonsteroidal anti-inflammatory drugs.

If you are at risk for an ulcer, or have had a previous ulcer or stomach bleed, your doctor may consider prescribing a newer class of NSAIDs. These are known as Cox-2 inhibitors (Table 5-2). The Cox-2 inhibitors may lower the risk of having severe stomach problems. These NSAIDs are equally effective as the traditional NSAIDs in decreasing pain and inflammation. However, both may affect kidney function and raise blood pressure. You and your doctor will want to carefully discuss the use of a Cox-2 inhibitor as the US Food and Drug Administration continues to closely monitor many of them.

Table 5-2: Cox-2 Inhibitor

Generic Name	Trade Name
Celecoxib	Celebrex®

Recent information raises the question of whether NSAIDs, including Cox-2 inhibitors, are associated with an increased risk of heart attacks in certain groups at high risk for heart problems.

What are steroids?

Steroids are strong inflammation fighters that your doctor can prescribe to help fight the inflammation of rheumatoid arthritis (Table 5-3). These are *not* the same steroids that are abused by some athletes. These steroids are naturally produced by your adrenal glands—a gland located near your kidneys. Steroid medicines can be given by mouth or by injection into a vein, muscle, or joint.

Table 5-3: Some Common Names of Steroids

Generic Name	Trade Name
Betamethasone	Celestone®
Cortisone	Cortone®
Dexamethasone	Decadron®
Hydroxycortisone	Hydrocortone®
Prednisone*	Deltasone®, Orasone®
Prednisolone	Delta-cortef®
Methylprednisolone*	Medrol®
Triamcinolone	Aristocort®

*Most frequently used.

If your doctor does prescribe steroid pills, always take the prescribed dose. Your body needs a certain amount of steroids each day. If you suddenly change your steroid dose by increasing, decreasing, skipping doses, or stopping your steroid pills, you may become very ill. *Take only the amount your doctor prescribes.* Your doctor knows the best way to change your steroid medicine without causing either a flare-up of your illness or sickness from sudden steroid loss.

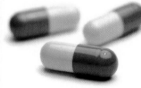

Do steroids have side effects?

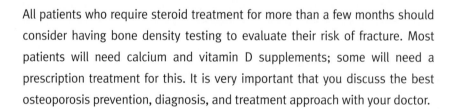

Low doses of steroids are less likely to cause severe side effects. However, the higher the steroid dose or the longer time you have been taking the medication, the greater the risk of side effects. Side effects include a round face ("moon face"), weight gain, high blood pressure, diabetes, bruising, cataracts, acne, emotional sensitivity, infections, and an increased risk of osteoporosis. There are steps you can take to reduce the risk of side effects. Avoid weight gain, limit the number of calories eaten, avoid high fat foods, avoid concentrated sweets, reduce salt intake, ensure adequate calcium and vitamin D intake, and exercise regularly.

All patients who require steroid treatment for more than a few months should consider having bone density testing to evaluate their risk of fracture. Most patients will need calcium and vitamin D supplements; some will need a prescription treatment for this. It is very important that you discuss the best osteoporosis prevention, diagnosis, and treatment approach with your doctor.

Steroids may be given as an injection into the joint. This can be a helpful, although temporary, treatment for a swollen painful joint.

You've now discussed medications that I recognize because they can treat many conditions. Isn't there a medication that is specifically for rheumatoid arthritis?

The medications we just discussed—although they can be used for many other conditions—are good for helping rheumatoid arthritis. However, SAARDs do decrease inflammation and slow arthritis down (Table 5-4).

Table 5-4: SAARDs

Generic Name	Trade Name	Form	Applicable For	Comments
hydroxychloroquine	Plaquenil®	pill	mild RA	older med
leflunomide	Arava®	pill	moderate/ severe RA	newer med
methotrexate	Rheumatrex®	pill or injection	moderate/ severe RA	older med
sulfasalazine	Azulfidine®	pill	mild/ moderate RA	older med
etanercept	Enbrel®	injection under skin	moderate/ severe RA	biologic med
adalimumab	Humira®	injection under skin	moderate/ severe RA	biologic med
infliximab	Remicade®	injection in the veins	moderate/ severe RA	biologic med
abatacept	Orencia®	injection in the veins	moderate/ severe RA	biologic med

SAARDs=slow-acting anti-rheumatic drugs.

SAARDs are stronger medicines that decrease inflammation and act on the body's cells to slow arthritis. Some also help suppress an overactive immune system, which can cause damage and keep the arthritis active. There are many types of SAARDs, and they vary in the way they fight arthritis. They may also have different side effects. The desired effect of all of these medications is to slow your rheumatoid arthritis before it causes permanent joint damage or deformity. All SAARDs are slow acting—you must take the correct dose for several months to determine how helpful it is for you. The dose varies for each of these medicines.

The newest class of SAARDs are biologic agents. These medicines reduce one type of molecule (called a cytokine) or immune cell communication, giving them a very specific way of treating rheumatoid arthritis. By reducing cytokine levels or immune cell communication, biologic SAARDs help to reduce pain, swelling, fatigue, stiffness and joint damage. Biologic SAARDs typically require an injection under the skin or into a vein.

What are the side effects of SAARDs?

Side effects vary by type of medication and the dose you are taking, but may include stomach discomfort, rash, dizziness, headache, weakness, skin rash, diarrhea, loss of appetite, elevations of liver enzymes, hair loss, birth defects, shortness of breath, infections, and eye problems (rare). Although rare, there have been reports of death due to liver problems with some SAARDs and so liver blood tests are required with certain agents. Methotrexate may very rarely associated with certain blood disorders and blood cell tumors (lymphoma).

Many more biologic SAARDs are being studied, but they are difficult to produce and are therefore very expensive. Possible side effects include pain, redness, warmth at the injection site, and an increased risk of infection. Certain biologic SAARDs may be very rarely associated with lymphoma, or reactivation (waking up) of previous tuberculosis. You should ask your physician about other serious side effects.

SAARDs are the mainstay of treatment of rheumatoid arthritis, and are very important and helpful medicines. Potential side effects vary greatly depending on the SAARD chosen. It is very important that you and your doctor discuss the benefits and risks of these medicines — ask questions!

If my doctor prescribes or suggests that I take medication, do I have to take it all the time?

Take what your doctor prescribes or suggests, take only the prescribed or recommended doses, and don't change your regimen without talking to your doctor. Also, be organized. Know the name, dose, and time you are to take each medicine. List each medicine on a piece of paper so that you have your own medication list. Use this list to remind yourself to take your medicines at the proper time. Some people tape their medication list to their refrigerator to help them remember. After taking each dose, mark your calendar to remind yourself that you've already taken the pills for that day. For example, if you were to take pills at breakfast, lunch, dinner, and bedtime, you should have four check marks at the end of the day.

Is surgery an option for rheumatoid arthritis?

Sometimes. Some people with rheumatoid arthritis need joint replacement surgery. Joints are only replaced when the joint is severely damaged and the individual experiences severe pain and loss of function that can't be helped by other means. The decision to surgically replace a joint is made together by the doctor and the patient. Replacing a joint is not a cure for rheumatoid arthritis because rheumatoid arthritis affects the entire body. The disease process will still need to be controlled by medication, even after a joint is replaced.

The Arthritis Foundation prints a pamphlet and a book about joint surgery. Remember, surgery isn't for all people with rheumatoid arthritis. But if you wonder if surgery is an option for you, be sure to ask your doctor.

In addition to medication or surgery, what role do I play in treating my rheumatoid arthritis?

You can help reduce your pain by controlling your stress level, having a proper diet, and getting the proper exercise. These are all discussed in Chapters 6 through 9.

CHAPTER SIX

What Does the Mind Have to Do with Rheumatoid Arthritis?

Stress is a part of everyone's life. Though it is familiar to us, we don't always understand it and, if it gets out of control, it can cause many problems. We experience stress as we meet life's demands—work overload, the frustrations of illness or chronic pain, annoyances in our environment, or our own anxiety. This constant pressure has been shown to put wear and tear on our bodies just as constant use causes a machine to wear.

How can stress be related to rheumatoid arthritis?

People with arthritis experience all the normal pressures of everyday life. They often have the added stress of chronic pain, the need to adapt to physical limitations, and the expenses of medical care. People sometimes find themselves caught up in a cycle of stress that triggers pain that, in turn, triggers depression. This can lead to increased stress, with the cycle starting all over again.

But life in general can be stressful. How can I eliminate it?

You can begin to deal with the stress in your life by determining what is causing harmful stress. Decide what you can do to simplify your life so that you can eliminate some of these stresses. Develop goals that are meaningful to you. Try to concentrate on the positive aspects of your life. Make a list of simple things that bring you pleasure, like a hot cup of tea or coffee, a cool drink, the soothing touch of a gentle breeze, the beauty of a sunset, the smile of a loved one, or the kind act of a friend. Make sure you enjoy some of these pleasures every day and learn how to savor them.

Q / A Can relaxation make my rheumatoid arthritis go away?

Relaxation alone probably can't make your rheumatoid arthritis go away, but it can help. Learning to relax can help break the cycle of stress, pain, and depression. Many methods of relaxation exist that you can vary and adapt to your style.

Look for ways you can help yourself. Simplify the activity that causes you stress. Pace yourself. Allow time for you. Do the work you have to do, but allow yourself to relax and enjoy each day too.

Q / A Exactly what do you mean by relaxation and what are some specific relaxation techniques?

Relaxation is a positive coping strategy. It can help you feel less anxious, help you better accept yourself, and help you feel calm and experience less pain.

Practice the following relaxation response once or twice each day for 15–20 minutes each time. Prepare to relax by following these steps:

- Find a quiet place to practice
- Sit or lay in a comfortable position
- Loosen clothing so nothing feels tight

Now, concentrate on repeating one word or sound or listen to soft soothing music. Mentally picture your favorite vacation or relaxation spot. Imagine what you see, hear, smell, and feel. Enjoy your mental vacation! If other thoughts enter your mind, just let them fade away.

What else can I do to relax?

You can take care of yourself physically, emotionally, intellectually, socially, and spiritually. Here are some tips:

- Physical exercise regularly
- Rest periodically during the day
- Eat healthy foods; drink 6 to 8 glasses of water daily (unless medically advised not to)
- Maintain a correct weight for your size
- Omit or limit alcohol consumption
- Don't smoke
- Visit your doctor regularly

Emotional

- Allow yourself to feel and express emotions, whether it is anger, sadness, happiness, or fear
- Respectfully resolve conflict
- Improve your self-awareness, nurture yourself and treat yourself well
- Don't take yourself too seriously
- Work off anger with physical exercise
- Say "No" when you want or need to

Intellectual

- Learn more about your disease and its treatment
- Ask questions of your doctor and other health professionals
- Learn and use self-help methods
- Consider participating in support groups

Social

- Develop and use support systems—talk with family and friends
- Start a hobby or become more engaged in a current hobby
- Take time off to vacation
- Limit the amount of time you spend watching television (or watch television with others)

- Engage in creative pastimes
- Enjoy intimacy
- Play with children
- Go out to entertaining events

Spiritual
- Use prayer or meditation (as a religious or nonreligious practice)
- "Let go" of unsolvable problems; take one day at a time and "flow" with the events of life
- Try communing with nature
- Read inspirational prose or poetry
- Appreciate the beauty of music and other arts
- Do something for another person

Relax!
Taking care of yourself in each of these ways can east the pain of rheumatoid arthritis
- Physical
- Emotional
- Intellectual
- Social
- Spiritual

The previous list was adapted from the book *Survival Skills for the New Nurse* by Jane Meyer Hamilton and Mary E. Kiefer.

CHAPTER SEVEN

What Does Diet Have to Do with Rheumatoid Arthritis?

Eating a well-balanced, healthy diet is important for people with rheumatoid arthritis. You may also have to make modifications depending on any medication you might take for your condition. If you have any questions, you should ask your doctor and dietitian.

Do I have to eat differently if I have rheumatoid arthritis?

Not necessarily. A healthy diet is based on variety, balance, and moderation. The latest food guide pyramid (Figure 7-1) developed by the US Department of Agriculture in 2005 provides a guide to eating a healthy diet based on choices from every food group and your balance between food and activity level. Most people should have at least the minimum number of servings suggested for each food group. Because of their body size and activity level, some people may need more servings. The following guidelines form the building blocks of a healthy meal plan:

- Eat a variety of foods and avoid those that may interact with your medications (this is discussed later in this chapter)
- Maintain a healthy weight
- Eat fat and cholesterol in moderation
- Eat plenty of vegetables, fruits, and whole grain products
- Use sugar and salt in moderation
- Discuss alcohol usage with your physician
- Take in the daily requirements of vitamins and minerals (including calcium)

Figure 7-1. The new Food Guide Pyramid developed by the US Department of Agriculture in 2005 offers general nutritional guidelines, but can be tailored to your nutritional requirements, based on age, gender, and activity level. You can go to <http://www.mypyramid.gov> to see how the pyramid can be tailored to you.

If you have rheumatoid arthritis, it may be difficult to prepare food because you may have joint pain, swelling, limited movement, and tiredness. Some medications you take may decrease your appetite or cause stomach and intestinal problems. If it's hard to follow a well-balanced diet, discuss this with your doctor.

Should I lose weight if I have rheumatoid arthritis?

Maintaining a healthy weight is important for everyone. However, an added benefit for people with arthritis is that a healthy weight reduces stress on the joints. People with rheumatoid arthritis may tend to gain weight because they are less mobile, eat for comfort, eat more fast foods that are high in calories and fat, and take steroid medications. Fresh fruits and whole grain breads and cereals provide more good nutrients than sweets (and can actually satisfy your sweet tooth). If you need to lose weight, ask for a dietitian's help in planning a diet that will work for you.

Do the medications I take have a relationship to the food I eat?

Steroid therapy, although a very beneficial treatment for certain types of arthritis, can change how the body uses sugar, protein, and salt. Some people may experience sugar intolerance and will benefit from controlling their carbohydrate intake. A good diet should include limiting concentrated sweets (like sugar-sweetened sodas, pies, cakes, and doughnuts). Steroids may also cause the body to lose potassium and retain salt. Limiting salt is recommended, so you should avoid the following:

- Salted and smoked meats (eg, bacon, bologna, hot dogs, ham, kielbasa, luncheon meats, sausage)
- Foods prepared in salt (sauerkraut, pickles, olives)
- Salted snack items (chips, pretzels, popcorn, crackers)
- Bouillon cubes, seasoned salts, seasoned sauces (soy, Worcestershire, chili sauce)
- Canned vegetables
- Canned or dried soups
- Cheese

You can substitute other spices for salt. Try pepper, garlic powder, onion powder, and basil.

To increase potassium, eat bananas, cantaloupes, prunes and prune juice, potatoes, tomatoes (fresh, sauces, and juice), and dried beans (baked beans, lima beans, split peas).

Antacids that reduce stomach irritation may also affect nutrients in the body. They contain high levels of sodium, calcium, and magnesium. Talk to your doctor before using antacids (or any type of vitamin, mineral, or herbal supplement).

Certain medications may cause constipation. Foods high in fiber (fresh fruits, vegetables, and whole grain breads and cereals) will help avoid constipation. It is also important to drink plenty of fluids—at least eight 8-ounce cups of water or liquid each day (unless otherwise directed by a doctor).

A person taking arthritis medications may experience diarrhea. To help control diarrhea, drink plenty of liquids to prevent dehydration and limit the amount of fiber in your diet. Some people also benefit from limiting dairy products. If you have diarrhea for more than a few days, notify your doctor.

I've seen advertisements that will boost my immune system. Do these work?

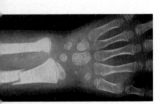

When a person has a chronic disease (such as rheumatoid arthritis), it is very tempting to look for a magical diet, food, or food supplement that claim to cure the disease. These claims are advertised on TV, the Internet, and in magazines and books. Unfortunately, most have not been scientifically tested to determine if they are beneficial (or even safe). Some diets are known to have harmful side effects—those with large doses of alfalfa, copper salts, or zinc, the so-called "immune power diet," or any plan that is very low in calories, fat, carbohydrates, or proteins.

CHAPTER EIGHT

What Does Exercise Have to Do with Rheumatoid Arthritis?

Exercise is muscle activity that helps us maintain fitness and is important for everyone! People with rheumatoid arthritis should exercise on a regular basis. When you have rheumatoid arthritis, though, it is important to know what exercises to do and how to do them. Sometimes motivation to exercise is hard when you feel stiff and sore, so included at the end of this chapter are exercises that are good for those with rheumatoid arthritis.

Should I exercise if I have rheumatoid arthritis?

Yes. What is the value of exercise? The benefits include the following:

- Increase your strength and flexibility
- Decrease stiffness
- Have less pain
- Become more active and less tired
- Strengthen your heart and increase circulation
- Find it easier to control your weight
- Increase nutrition to all parts of your body
- Feel good!

Q
A Do people with rheumatoid arthritis have to exercise any differently?

Yes. Here are some tips.

Plan Ahead

Select the same time each day to exercise. Choose the time of day you usually feel best. If you have rheumatoid arthritis, you probably wake up stiff and need a little more preparation time than most people before exercising.

Warm Up

If you have rheumatoid arthritis, you should physically warm up just before exercising. Take a warm bath or shower or warm up stiff and sore joints with hot packs. Warming up helps you reduce stiffness, increase circulation, and relax muscles. If you have an extremely painful, swollen joint, try an ice pack on it. Some people with arthritis use ice first and then heat swollen areas before beginning their exercise.

Do Gentle Stretches, Slowly and Smoothly

Gentle stretches are also called *range of motion* exercises. Stretch your arms and legs and move all parts of your body in the direction they were made to go. Move slowly and smoothly. Try not to use quick, jerky movements. Give your body time to feel each gentle stretch. This time is important for you to evaluate how you are doing during exercise. If you have increased pain during exercise, change the exercise you are doing or the length of time you do it. If, after 1 or 2 hours of exercising you experience a lot more pain than you had before you exercised, taper back the amount of exercise the next day. It's much better to gradually build up your exercise amount.

Do Aerobic Exercise for Fun and Health

Even though you have arthritis, you should continue to do fun activities that will also gradually raise your heart rate and metabolism. It might be easier and more enjoyable if you select activities with less resistance like walking, swimming, dancing, or riding a bike. Activities that require bouncing, pounding, or jerky movements (such as jogging, jumping rope, playing tennis, or heavy contact sports like football or soccer) may be harder and more painful. If you aren't certain what exercises to do, ask your doctor or physical therapist.

Always Do Cool-Down Exercises

When you've finished exercising, remember that it's important to gradually slow down, rather than abruptly stop. You can walk in place 2 or 3 minutes or repeat a few gentle stretches. End your exercise by taking deep breaths in through your nose and out slowly through your mouth. This will gradually allow your heart rate to return to normal.

The Basics of Exercise
- Plan ahead
- Warm up
- Cool down
- Relax!

Relax After You Exercise

If you can, lay down for 15–20 minutes after exercising. Relax and enjoy the sensation after exercising. You will see how much better you feel!

What exercises are appropriate for people with rheumatoid arthritis?

Exercises can be classified as those for the following:

- Upper extremities
- Spine, chest, and trunk
- Lower extremities

To develop your own individual program, you might begin by selecting a few exercises from each of the three categories and gradually add others. Consult your doctor, physical or occupational therapist, rheumatologist, or rehabilitation nurse specialist.

When you do the stretching exercises, begin with just a few exercises and gradually add other stretches. Stretch just to the point where it begins to feel tight. Hold it for 3 to 5 seconds, then relax.

Upper Extremities

Hands.   In general, use the heel of the palm of your hand when pushing down, such as when using hands to help you get up from a chair. Also, always be gentle with your thumbs—they are essential for hand function. As you do these exercises, watch your fingers as you exercise them. Avoid putting pressure in the direction of joint deformity or toward your little finger. Unless otherwise specified, repeat each exercise 3 to 5 times (Figures 8-1 to 8-4).

Figure 8-1. Gently touch the tip of the thumb to the tip of each finger forming an "O" with your fingers.

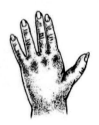

Figure 8-2. Bring two fingers together. Repeat with each of the other fingers of both hands.

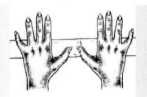

Figure 8-3. With both palms facing each other, shape an exercise putty (you can get Theraputty® through your occupational therapist or buy it in most sport shops) into a log. Roll back and forth from heel to palm to tips of fingers. Fold log and repeat.

Figure 8-4. Lightly touch each fingertip to the palm of hand then release.

Wrists. It won't help you if your fingers stay flexible but your wrists aren't! Work them whenever you exercise your fingers (Figure 8-5).

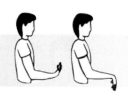

Figure 8-5. With palm facing down, bend your wrist up as far as possible. Then slowly bend wrist down. Work both sides equally

Elbows. By exercising your elbows, you pave the way for more flexible arm movements (Figure 8-6).

Figure 8-6. With your arm straight at your side, bend elbow and touch your shoulder. Return to starting position. Work both sides equally

Wall "Walking". These exercises work the whole arm—from shoulder through elbow, wrists, and fingers. Standing facing wall (Figure 8-7). Standing sideways (Figure 8-8).

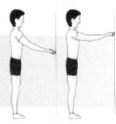

Figure 8-7. Stand facing wall. Walk fingers up wall keeping elbows as straight as possible. Reach as far as possible. Return to starting position. Work both sides equally.

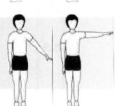

Figure 8-8. Stand sideways with the affected shoulder towards wall. Slowly walk fingers up the wall keeping your elbow as straight as possible. Reach as far as possible. Return to starting position. Work both sides equally.

Towel Exercise. It's good to perform exercises that mimic actual positions that you might use during the course of a day. You might use the motions for this one after bathing or showering (Figure 8-9).

Figure 8-9. Hold towel behind you with one hand up over shoulder and other hand at hip, pull towel back and forth slowly as if drying your back

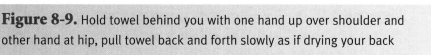

Spine, Chest, and Trunk

Neck. You should be careful to perform only neck exercises that your doctor or physical therapist has prescribed (Figures 8-10 to 8-13).

Figure 8-10. Rotation. Turn your head to the right as if you are looking over your shoulder. Keep chin level. Do not tilt your head. Repeat to opposite side. Hold 5 to 10 seconds.

Figure 8-11. Side tilt. Slowly tilt head with left ear pointing toward left shoulder. Return to starting position with head erect. Then slowly tilt right ear toward right shoulder. Hold 5 to 10 seconds.

Figure 8-12. Cervical spine. Forward bend. Bend your head forward and let it rest with your chin near your chest. Hold 5 to 10 seconds

Figure 8-13. While sitting, use one hand to grasp the other arm above the wrist and pull downward and across body while gently tilting head. Look down and away. Do slowly in a gentle stretch. Hold 5 to 10 seconds.

Lifts. Any time you lift something over your head, a lying or sitting posture is best so that you don't lose your balance (Figure 8-14).

Figure 8-14. Lying flat on the floor (or while sitting), place a ruler (or item of similar shape and size) in both hands and lift it over your head. Keep your elbows straight as you do this.

Shoulder Shrugs.   It's especially challenging in this exercise to engage only your shoulders—and keep the arms as relaxed as possible (Figure 8-15).

Figure 8-15. While sitting or standing, shrug shoulders, hold for a count of five, and then relax. Do both shoulders at the same time. Keep arms relaxed at sides

Shoulder Rolls.   Rotating the shoulders engages more than just the shoulders—you can feel the arms and back working, too (Figure 8-16).

Figure 8-16. While sitting or standing and with arms relaxed at your sides, make circular motions with the tips of your shoulders—first in one direction and then in the other.

Bending (forward).   Bends are good for trunk flexibility, but sitting ensures that you won't lose your balance (Figure 8-17).

Figure 8-17. While seated, gently bend forward at the waist reaching toward the floor. Return to upright position and then pull shoulders back.

Bending (sideways).   When bending sideways from a sitting position, use a chair with armrests so that you don't lose your balance—just be sure that the armrests aren't too high or you won't get the benefit of the bending (Figure 8-18).

Figure 8-18. While seated, gently lean to one side bending at the waist. Return to starting position and then lean to opposite side.

Trunk Rotation.   Twists are good for flexibility. Make sure your head moves along with your rotating movement (Figure 8-19).

Figure 8-19. While seated, gently rotate your trunk to the right. Return to starting position and then rotate slowly toward the left.

Lower extremities

Knees. Your knees connect the bottom of your trunk to the ground so you'll want to be sure to try to keep them in good condition (Figure 8-20).

Figure 8-20. Sitting on a chair with foot flat on floor, slowly raise foot off floor and straighten knee. Hold for 2 seconds and return to starting position. Repeat both sides.

Ankles. You'll see the benefits of keeping the ankles flexible when you walk (Figure 8-21).

Figure 8-21. Slowly pull foot up at ankle and then push down at ankle. Make large, slow circles with feet in each direction. Make sure movement is at ankle. Use big toe as pointer. Repeat with each foot.

Hips. Your hips are really the key to your trunk. They help you balance and stand firmly (Figures 8-22 to 8-24).

Figure 8-22. Lying on the floor, keep right leg flat and pull left leg up, bending at the knee and hip. Return to the starting position. Repeat with right leg keeping left leg flat.

Figure 8-23. Lying on the floor, pull legs apart keeping knees straight. Return to starting position.

Figure 8-24. Lying flat on your stomach, lift leg up keeping hips down and knee straight. Slowly return to starting position. Repeat with opposite leg.

Thighs. The thighs contain the largest muscles in the legs so they are used to working the hardest. Try to keep the rest of your body relaxed while you do these exercises (Figure 8-25).

Figure 8-25. While lying on your back, straighten your knee by pushing your knee down and tightening the muscle on top of your leg. Hold for a count of five. Relax.

Buttocks. The good thing about exercising your buttocks is you can do it practically anywhere—and no one will even know (Figure 8-26)!

Figure 8-26. Lie on the floor with your legs straight. Squeeze your buttocks together. Hold for a count of five. Relax and then repeat.

Breathing

Being good at and diligently doing all the exercises listed here won't help unless you breathe deeply and correctly. You should always try to be mindful of your breathing (Figure 8-27).

Figure 8-27. Lie flat on the floor with hands on the sides of your chest. Inhale deeply and push your ribs out against your hands. Hold 2 seconds and then breathe out through your mouth. Remember, posture is important.

How do I know if I've overdone my exercise?

The Arthritis Foundation recommends you use the following pain rules to guide you in all your activities:

- If you have an increase in pain while exercising, taper back or skip that particular exercise, but don't stop exercising completely.
- If you experience increased arthritis pain 2 or more hours after the activity than before, then it was too much for you. Next time, taper the amount of exercise time back–but never completely stop all exercise or activity.

CHAPTER NINE

Living with Rheumatoid Arthritis

Fatigue is common with a chronic disease such as rheumatoid arthritis, especially when the arthritis flares up. People who have rheumatoid arthritis commonly have difficulties when performing daily activities, such has dressing and undressing, bathing, going to the bathroom, walking, getting up from a chair, reaching, cooking, and buying and wearing shoes. This chapter will discuss these problem areas and offer some solutions. Also, many devices can assist with daily life. Consult medical-surgical companies, pharmacies, arthritis specialty companies, and department and hardware stores for assistive devices and arthritis self-help equipment.

I have problems dressing and undressing. What can I do to make those tasks easier for me?

Problem: One of your arms is more painful and cannot reach as far as the other arm.

Solution: Place the more painful arm in your shirt or blouse sleeve first. Then place the other arm in the other sleeve. When removing the clothing, take the less painful arm out of the sleeve first. The same will work for a painful or less mobile leg.

The Four "Ps" of Rheumatoid Arthritis

Plan—Eliminate wasted body motion. Make lists of what needs to be done and then work efficiently.

Prioritize—Organize tasks in order of importance.

Pace—Balance rest and activity. Do a heavy job, then a lighter job, and then take a rest. Try completing harder tasks in stages rather than all in one day.

Protect

- Protect joints while performing a task, making the task easier and more comfortable.
- Reduce the force necessary to accomplish a task. Use handles on a toothbrush or pencil so that you don't need to squeeze as tightly to hold onto it.
- Use the largest joint possible to accomplish the task. For instance, carry your purse on your forearm or shoulder instead of holding in your hands.
- Use equipment to help you. An electric can opener is easier on your joints than the hand-held openers that require twisting.

Simplify Your Work

- How many trips did you make to do the job? Could you reduce that number? Could you simplify the order?
- Are materials and equipment within easy reach? Do storage areas only contain materials you need?
- Can you omit or change any part of the task?
- Do you use good body mechanics in posture, sitting, standing, and lifting?
- Do you use two hands to the best advantage?
- Would using wheels be helpful?
- Are chairs comfortable and at the proper height?
- Are you working at too quickly a pace?
- Should someone else do part (or all) of the task?

Problem: You can' t button buttons.

Solutions:

- Use Velcro closures. You can buy these at sewing centers and variety stores and then add them to your clothes. Some stores sell clothing with Velcro closures for easy dressing.
- Buy clothes with large buttons and holes.
- Use a special device (sometimes called a "buttoner" or a "button hook") to help manage your buttons (Figure 9-1).

Figure 9-1. Button hook.

Problem: You can' t hook your bra.

Solutions:

- Turn bra around and hook in front first and then turn back around to fit properly.
- Velcro closures may work for some smaller-breasted women. You can buy specially made bras that have large hooks and easy to pull closure loops in some undergarment stores and department stores.
- Replace zippers with Velcro strips.

Problem: It' s hard to grasp zipper tabs.

Solution: Use a special device called a "zipper pull" to open or close zippers (Figure 9-2).

Figure 9-2. Zipper pull.

Q My rheumatoid arthritis makes bathing difficult. What can help?

A Problem: *You have difficulty getting in and out of the tub.*

Solutions:

- Place grab bar on inside wall of bath tub or over tub's outside edge.
- Put non-skid treads on the bottom of your tub.
- Sit on a small stool or bench while in the tub.
- Use a hand-held shower head.
- Shower standing in a shower stall that has a low edge and doesn't require you to step up very high to get in it.
- Use soap-on-a-rope or put soap in a wash mitt.
- Use a long-handled sponge for difficult-to-reach body areas.

Q Even going to the bathroom can be difficult. What can I do to make it easier?

A Problem: *You have difficulty getting up from or sitting down on the toilet.*

Solutions:

- Place a grab bar diagonally on the wall next to the toilet. Have the grab bar mounted with the lowest end nearest the toilet and the highest end away from the toilet. This will help you move from sitting to standing position (and vice versa).
- Buy an elevated toilet seat at your local medical/surgical company, pharmacy, or department store. Plastic ones that fit into the toilet bowl work well.

Q Are there any tips for walking when you have rheumatoid arthritis?

A Problem: *You have pain when you walk.*

Solutions:

- Pace yourself. Walk, then sit; walk, then sit. Walk only as far as you know you will be able to return.
- Walk on paved, level ground.
- Consider using a cane or walker. Before using a cane or walker, talk to a physical therapist.

Do I need to wear special shoes if I have rheumatoid arthritis?

Problem: It's hard to buy shoes that provide proper support, control deformity, and offer maximum comfort.

Solutions:

- Select shoes that provide sufficient room in the toe area.
- Avoid shoes that push the toes inward or place pressure on the top of the toes.
- Shoes with enough depth and width can help prevent the toes from pointing in or out.
- A soft insert placed in the shoes can help relieve pain in areas such as the ball of the foot.

- Select shoes with low heels (one inch or less). Prolonged use of high heels may cause the calf muscles to shorten and can affect posture, placing harmful stress on the spine.
- Make sure your shoe has an adequate arch that distributes weight evenly.
- Use shoes with a firm heel counter (the insert that reinforces the heel of a shoe and increases stability).
- If you have deformities in the toes, it is recommended that you put material in the top of the shoe. This helps prevent open sores and calluses from developing.
- Your physician might recommend other shoe modifications or even custom-made and "extra-depth" shoes. You can buy these through an orthopedic shoe specialist.

Do you have tips for getting up from a seated position?

Problem: You have difficulty moving from sitting to standing.

Solutions:

- When you can, sit in higher seats and firmer chairs.
- Use a chair with arms on both sides. This will help you push yourself out of the chair.
- Move to the edge of the seat before you try to stand. Plant your feet firmly on the floor. Rock forward to stand.

Q Stairs present a challenge to me with my rheumatoid arthritis. What can I do?

A *Problem: It's hard to go up or down stairs.*
Solutions:

- When they are available, use handrails on each side, but at least one side rail will help.
- Take one step at a time so both feet are on the same step before you move to the next step. Hold the rail as you go.
- If you find it difficult going downstairs, try coming down facing the rail.
- Come down the steps in a sitting position, holding onto the rail.

Q What should I do if I have trouble reaching things?

A *Problem: Reaching objects is difficult.*
Solution: Check hardware or variety stores (or use your imagination) to make a long-handled "reacher." Ask an occupational therapist for suggestions.

Q I have to cook but my rheumatoid arthritis makes it difficult. What can make it easier?

A *Problem: It is difficult to lift pots and pans.*
Solutions:

- Use a strainer in a larger pot so you only have to lift the strainer with the food (rather than the food and the water).
- When lifting, use two hands. Wear a mitt on one hand to support the bottom of the pot and hold the pot handle with the other hand.

Problem: It is difficult to open jars and cans.

Solutions:

- Use a rubber pad or wear a rubber glove to provide traction when twisting a jar lid open.
- Use an electric can opener.
- Purchase a product that allows you to twist the jar open with two hands while the lid is held in place. You can buy this type of product at a local hardware or variety store or through an arthritis equipment catalog (Figure 9-3).

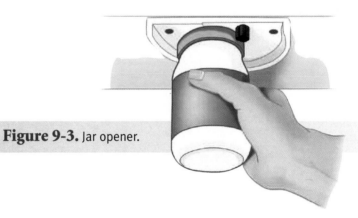

Figure 9-3. Jar opener.

CHAPTER TEN

Where Can I Get Help?

Community resources are available to help people with chronic health problems. A social worker can help identify which community services are available in your area. Ask your doctor, nurse, therapist, or call your local hospital or home health agency for assistance.

Having rheumatoid arthritis has caused me much financial stress. Is there anywhere I can get help?

Financial stress is a common result of chronic illness. Government assistance programs include disability, supplemental security income (SSI), and cash assistance.

- Disability is managed by the Social Security Administration. This program helps support individuals and their families when the primary financial provider is unable to work for 1 year or longer.
- SSI is managed by the Social Security Administration with funds coming from income taxes. This program is for persons who are aged, disabled, or blind, and have very little income.
- Cash assistance can be obtained through the Department of Public Assistance.

What about my medical costs? Can I get help paying those?

There's a good chance that you can.

- People over the age of 65 (and some disabled persons under the age of 65) can receive help through the government insurance program (Medicare). Medicare is an insurance program covering hospital costs and outpatient costs. Apply for Medicare through the Social Security Office.

- Medicaid (or Medical Assistance) is designed to help people of any age who have low income but need basic health care. Levels of coverage vary depending on the financial situation. Medicaid covers such things as hospital care, physician visits, laboratory costs, and nursing home costs. Apply through the Office of Public Assistance.

Private insurances and health maintenance organizations also provide valuable health services. You can contact them directly to find out what services they provide.

What if I have day-to-day needs? Can I get help with those?

There are agencies that help people with day-to-day needs. These include visiting nurses, Offices on Aging, and offices for adult services. Visiting nurse services are private agencies whose costs are covered by private insurance, Medicare, or Medicaid (if ordered by a doctor). These agencies are usually able to offer skilled nursing, home health aids, occupational or physical therapy, and medical social work to homebound patients.

Most counties have Area Agency on Aging Offices that offer many services to people over the age of 60. These are government-supported offices and case workers are able to make home visits to help determine a person's need. The Area Agency on Aging Offices oversee programs such as Meals-on-Wheels, senior center meals and activities, adult day care, Lifeline telephone communication, transportation assistance, Pharmaceutical Assistance Contract for the Elderly (PACE) medication assistance applications, attendant care programs, respite care programs, and homemaker services. Contact your county Area Agency on Aging to discuss your needs with a caseworker. Most counties also have an Office of Transportation to assist disabled people under age 60.

Are there organizations that can help me learn about and understand rheumatoid arthritis?

The Arthritis Foundation of America is a private voluntary agency that specifically helps people with arthritis. The Arthritis Foundation sponsors several educational programs, such as the *Arthritis Self-Help Course* and public forums to help people learn to manage day-to-day living with arthritis. They also provide educational pamphlets and books and publish a magazine called *Arthritis Today*. They also have a recommended book list of excellent resources. Contact the Arthritis Foundation at 1-800-283-7800 or on the Internet at <www.arthritis.org>.

Q

A

The Arthritis Foundation

1-800-283-7800

Glossary

Analgesics are pain relief medications.

Anti-cyclic citrullinated peptide is a relatively new test that may indicate rheumatoid arthritis. It can be detected in patients even before the rheumatoid factor becomes positive.

Arthritis is any condition that changes the joint or interferes with joint motion.

Autoimmune disease (such as rheumatoid arthritis) is so named because if you have rheumatoid arthritis, your immune system mistakes your body's healthy tissue for a foreign invader and attacks it.

Blood rheumatoid factor is an antibody that is not usually present in a normal individual but is often elevated in people with rheumatoid arthritis.

Contrast bath is the use of 10 minutes of cold followed by 10 minutes of heat applied to swollen, painful joints.

Inflammation is your body's way of protecting itself and helping heal an injured area.

Inflammatory arthritis means the joints, the lining of the joint, and surrounding tissues are inflamed.

Noninflammatory arthritis is a condition caused from cartilage becoming worn down. O*steoarthritis* (degenerative joint disease) is the most common form.

Nonsteroidal anti-inflammatory drugs (NSAIDs) are medications used to decrease arthritis symptoms—pain and inflammation.

Range of motion exercises are gentle stretches that are good for people with rheumatoid arthritis to do.

Rheumatoid arthritis is the most common form of inflammatory arthritis. It is a *chronic* disease—one that lasts for a long time. Signs and symptoms include stiffness, fatigue, pain, limited joint motion, joint swelling, and warm and red joints.

Rheumatologist is the doctor best trained to diagnose and treat rheumatoid arthritis; a specialist in *rheumatology*.

Slow-acting anti-rheumatic drugs (SAARDs) are medications that decrease inflammation and slow arthritis down.

Steroids (corticosteroids) are medications that are strong inflammation fighters.